A Men's Guide to Spiritual Warfare

Daily Prayers to Overcome Anxiety, Loneliness, and Spiritual Attacks with God's Strength and Peace

Faith Linwood

© Copyright 2025 by Faith Linwood. All Rights Reserved.

This publication is intended for informational purposes only. It does not offer legal, medical, or professional advice. Readers should consult a qualified professional when needed. While every effort has been made to provide accurate and reliable content, the publisher assumes no responsibility for errors, omissions, or the outcomes of applying the information contained herein.

No part of this book may be reproduced, stored, or transmitted in any form or by any means, electronic, mechanical, or otherwise, without the prior written permission of the publisher. All rights reserved.

Any trademarks mentioned are the property of their respective owners and are used solely for identification and clarification. This publication is not affiliated with or endorsed by those trademark holders.

Table of Contents

(Exclusive bonuses at the end of the book)

Chapter 1 – A Call to Spiritual War............1

1.1 What It Means to Be a Man at War 1
1.2 The Real Enemy: Spiritual Battles in Everyday Life.. 3
1.3 Why Prayer Is Your First Weapon 5
1.4 How to Use This Book for Daily Strength 7

Chapter 2 – Daily Warfare Prayers 10

Section 1: Battles of the Mind 10
A Prayer Against Anxiety 10
A Prayer for Mental Clarity 11
A Prayer for Peace Over Racing Thoughts 12
A Prayer to Silence Fear 14
A Prayer for Rest and Renewal 15
Section 2: Temptation and Self-Control 16
A Prayer for Strength Against Sexual Sin 16
A Prayer for Self-Discipline......................................18
A Prayer for Victory Over Addiction 19
A Prayer to Resist Daily Temptation.......................21
A Prayer for Consistency in Holiness..................... 22
Section 3: Isolation and Loneliness 23
A Prayer for God's Nearness 23
A Prayer to Heal Inner Loneliness 25
A Prayer to Rebuild Brotherhood 26
A Prayer to Connect Authentically 27
A Prayer to Feel Seen and Known 29
Section 4: Family and Leadership........................... 30
A Prayer for Your Role as a Husband 30
A Prayer for Future Fatherhood or Father Healing 31

A Prayer to Lead Spiritually at Home 33
A Prayer to Break Generational Patterns 34
A Prayer for Unity and Peace in the Household 35
Section 5: Spiritual Fatigue and Pressure 36
A Prayer for Strength When You Feel Weak 36
A Prayer When You Feel Spiritually Dry 38
A Prayer for Patience Under Pressure 39
A Prayer for Focus and Mental Fortitude 40
A Prayer to Guard Your Peace at Work 42
Section 6: Direct Spiritual Warfare 43
A Prayer to Break Spiritual Strongholds 43
A Prayer to Cancel the Enemy's Assignment 44
A Prayer for Angelic Protection 45
A Prayer to Walk in Authority 47
A Prayer for Full Deliverance 48

Chapter 3 – Reflection and Spiritual Activation 50

3.1 Don't Just Pray, Listen 50
3.2 Journal Prompts for Men After Each Prayer 52

Standing Firm in Every Battle 55

Chapter 1 – A Call to Spiritual War

1.1 What It Means to Be a Man at War

Being a man in today's world means living under constant pressure. You are expected to be strong, steady, and in control. Yet deep down, there is a battle going on that most people around you do not see. It is not a fight with fists or weapons, but a spiritual war that is happening inside your mind, in your home, and around your everyday decisions. To be a man at war means recognizing that your faith, your peace, and your leadership are under attack—and choosing to fight back with the power God has given you.

This war is real. The enemy is not a person or a political system. It is not your boss, your spouse, or the culture. Scripture makes it clear that we do not wrestle against flesh and blood, but against spiritual forces that seek to kill your purpose, steal your peace, and destroy your identity as a man of God. When you feel anger boiling up for no clear reason, when temptation hits you in the quiet moments, when fear creeps in late at night or shame whispers in your ear, that is not just life, it is war.

But here is the good news. You are not fighting this war alone. God has equipped you with everything you need to overcome, stand firm, and lead with confidence. Through Christ, you already have access to spiritual authority. You have been called to stand in the gap for your family, to walk with boldness, and to speak life where there is darkness. Being a man at war means stepping into that calling with your eyes open, your mind alert, and your heart anchored in God's truth.

Men of faith are not passive. They do not sit back and hope things improve. They stand up, pray hard, and fight smart. They know that silence in the spirit leads to defeat in the flesh. That is why a man at war becomes a man of prayer. Every word you speak in prayer becomes a weapon against fear, anxiety, temptation, and confusion. You are not just asking for help, you are declaring your ground, building a shield around your home, and reminding the enemy that you belong to the living God.

This book exists because too many men feel overwhelmed and under-equipped. The pressures of life, the wounds of the past, and the silent battles within can make even the strongest man feel unqualified to lead spiritually. But this is your moment to step forward. God is not looking for perfect men. He is calling willing men, those who are ready to take prayer seriously, take their place in the fight, and live with purpose.

Being a man at war means guarding your heart, staying alert, and refusing to let fear or shame rule your life. It means showing up with your armor on, even on the days when you feel tired or uncertain. It means being real about your struggles, and even more real about your faith. Because the truth is, the more you pray, the stronger you get. The more you speak God's Word over your situation, the clearer your purpose becomes. And the more you take your place as a spiritual leader, the more you begin to see victory, not just for you, but for the people God has placed in your life.

This fight is not about proving yourself. It is about surrendering to the One who already won. To be a man at war is to walk in daily connection with God, armed with His truth and committed to standing your ground. You are not weak for needing help. You are wise for knowing where your help comes from. This is your battlefield. This is your calling. And it begins with prayer.

1.2 The Real Enemy: Spiritual Battles in Everyday Life

Most men know how to fight what they can see. If someone disrespects their family, they react. If their job is on the line, they push harder. If their body is in pain, they seek a solution. But the toughest battles are not physical. They are invisible, internal, and spiritual. These battles do not make noise, but they leave deep marks. They show up in moments of anger that feel out of control, in sudden feelings of worthlessness, in long nights of overthinking and in days filled with emptiness. This is not weakness. This is war. And it is time to recognize the real enemy.

The Bible is clear. You are not wrestling against flesh and blood. Your enemy is not your spouse, your coworkers, your friends, or even yourself. Your enemy is spiritual. He is strategic. He works through lies, distractions, confusion, and shame. His goal is to wear you down until you accept defeat as normal and stop praying altogether. That is the trap many men fall into. They think their tiredness is only physical, their frustration is just stress, their temptation is just natural. But beneath all of that is an invisible war aimed at stealing your faith and silencing your voice.

Spiritual battles happen everywhere. They show up at work when you feel pressure to compromise your integrity. They appear in your thoughts when you are reminded of old sins and feel condemned. They hit hard when you feel alone and start to believe no one truly understands you. These are not coincidences. These are moments of spiritual warfare. And if you do not know how to fight back, you will begin to believe lies that were never yours to carry.

The real enemy works through suggestion. He whispers things that sound like your own voice. Things like, "You are not good enough," "You always mess things up," "God is disappointed in you," "You will never change." These are not random thoughts. They are weapons meant to weaken your confidence in God and in yourself. If you do not recognize them for what they are, you begin to agree with them. And once agreement sets in, spiritual ground is lost.

But you do not have to lose. You have the right and the responsibility to fight back. You do that by identifying the lie and replacing it with truth. You fight by saying, "That is not who I am. That is not what God says. I choose to stand on His Word, not on this feeling." Every time you declare truth over a lie, you push darkness back. Every time you pray instead of panic, you step into your God-given authority.

The problem is that most men do not realize this battle is spiritual. They try to fix it in the natural. They isolate when they feel low. They bury pain instead of praying through it. They chase relief instead of rest. But nothing in the world can fix a problem that started in the spirit. Only God can restore what the enemy tried to break. And He does that through your willingness to fight with the weapons He has given you.

God did not leave you defenseless. You have His Word. You have prayer. You have the Holy Spirit. You have access to truth, authority, and power. But you must choose to use them. You must be alert. You must treat the subtle battles in your everyday life as real. Because they are.

This fight is not about fear. It is about awareness. When you learn to see the enemy's patterns, you begin to walk with wisdom. When you respond with prayer, you build a spiritual wall that cannot be shaken. The enemy may try to strike, but you will no longer be surprised. You will be ready. You will be steady. You will be strong.

The real battle is not somewhere out there. It is here, in your thoughts, your choices, your atmosphere. And it is not someone else's job to win it. It is yours. Stand up. Pay attention. Speak truth. And walk in the strength that God has already placed inside you.

1.3 Why Prayer Is Your First Weapon

When a man faces trouble, his first instinct is often to act. Fix it. Solve it. Push through it. That is what men are taught to do. But in spiritual warfare, the most powerful action you can take is not physical. It is spiritual. And it starts with prayer. Prayer is not a backup plan. It is not something you do after everything else has failed. It is your first weapon. It is your first move in the fight. Because it is the place where battles are won before they ever reach the surface.

Prayer is not weak. It is not passive. It is not quiet submission to whatever happens. Prayer is authority.

Prayer is access. Prayer is standing in the presence of God and declaring truth in the face of fear, confusion, temptation, and darkness. When you pray, you are not just speaking into the air. You are stepping into the most powerful connection a man can have, the direct line between you and the living God.

Every battle you face begins in the unseen. That is why your fight must begin in the unseen too. When Jesus was on Earth, He faced attacks, pressure, and temptation. But His response was always rooted in prayer. Before choosing His disciples, He prayed. When the crowd tried to crown Him, He slipped away to pray. Before going to the cross, He dropped to His knees and prayed with such intensity that His sweat became like blood. If Jesus treated prayer as His first weapon, how much more should we?

Many men struggle in silence because they are trying to win spiritual battles with natural tools. They try to outthink anxiety. They try to outwork spiritual fatigue. They try to avoid temptation with willpower alone. But the enemy is not intimidated by your effort. He is pushed back by your faith. And faith is activated in prayer.

When you pray, you open the door for God to move in areas where you feel stuck. You invite peace into places where fear tried to build a home. You allow heaven to interrupt the enemy's plan for your life. Prayer is not about feelings. It is about authority. Even when you feel weak, even when you feel unworthy, your prayer has weight because it is backed by the name of Jesus.

Prayer also builds awareness. The more you pray, the more clearly you see what is really happening around you. You stop reacting to the surface and start discerning the source. That is how spiritual warriors are built. Not in noise or performance, but in quiet moments of consistent connection with the Father. A praying man is a dangerous man to the enemy. Because a praying man is awake. A praying man is equipped. A praying man cannot be manipulated by lies.

If you are waiting to feel spiritual before you pray, the enemy has already disarmed you. Prayer is not for the perfect. It is for the willing. It is for the man who says, "God, I do not have all the answers, but I trust You more than I trust my own strength." That is what opens the door to breakthrough. Not long speeches. Not memorized words. Just honest, bold, faith-filled prayer.

In this book, you will be given words to start with. Prayers for real struggles. Prayers for real men. But the goal is not that you repeat them like a script. The goal is that your spirit wakes up. That you begin to speak life over your own situation. That you begin to pray not just for survival, but for victory.

This is your weapon. Use it first. Use it often. Use it without shame. Because when you pray, you are not stepping into weakness, you are stepping into your place as a man of God who refuses to fight alone. And that changes everything.

1.4 How to Use This Book for Daily Strength

This book is not meant to be read once and set aside. It is a tool. It is a weapon. It is a daily source of strength for men who are serious about standing firm in their faith and winning the battles that matter most. You do not need to read it cover to cover in one sitting. You need to return to it again and again, especially on the days when you feel the pressure building or the peace slipping. This is your manual for spiritual strength, and it is meant to be used that way.

Each prayer in this book has been crafted with purpose. The words are not random. They are specific. They are drawn from real battles that men face every day, battles in the mind, in the heart, in relationships, in temptation, in leadership, and in spiritual pressure. Every prayer is short enough to fit into a busy day but powerful enough to shift the atmosphere when spoken with faith. You are not just reading. You are engaging in a spiritual act that has the power to protect, restore, and renew.

The most important thing you can do with this book is to use it consistently. Do not wait until the pressure explodes. Make prayer your daily habit, not your last resort. Start your morning with one of the prayers. Speak it out loud. Say the words slowly. Let them sink into your mind and your spirit. Do not rush through them. If a phrase hits you, stop and repeat it. If a truth stands out, write it down. If a verse connects with your current situation, go look it up in your Bible and let it shape your thinking.

You can also keep this book with you during the day. Bring it to work. Leave it on your desk. Keep it in your car or in your bag. When stress hits, open to the prayer that matches your need. When temptation rises, flip to the section on self-control. When fear creeps in, pray the words that push it out. This book is not just for quiet time. It is for real time.

Another way to use this book is to speak the prayers over others. If you are a husband, speak them over your wife. If you are a father, declare them over your children. If you are single, speak them over your future family. You are called to be a spiritual covering, and that starts with prayer. Do not underestimate the power of your voice when you speak in agreement with God's Word. Your words carry spiritual weight. They create space for peace to enter, for strongholds to fall, and for the presence of God to move.

You can also return to the same prayer more than once. Some battles take time. Some wounds need layers of healing. Some patterns break only through repetition and persistence. If a specific prayer speaks to you, use it every day until you feel a shift. There is no rule that says you have to move on quickly. Real transformation takes time, and God honors the man who keeps showing up in prayer.

Finally, use the reflection section of this book to go deeper. After you pray, sit quietly. Ask God what He is saying. Write down what comes to mind. Be honest. Be real. These moments of listening are often where the biggest breakthroughs begin. Prayer is not just about speaking. It is also about receiving.

This book was written for men who want more than survival. It was written for men who want to lead, protect, and grow with God at the center. You are not weak for needing help. You are wise for using the tools God has given you. Keep this book close. Use it daily. Let it remind you that you are not powerless. You are a man of God. You are in a battle. And you are never fighting alone.

Chapter 2 – Daily Warfare Prayers

Section 1: Battles of the Mind

A Prayer Against Anxiety

"Cast all your anxiety on Him because He cares for you."
1 Peter 5:7

Sometimes anxiety creeps in quietly, and sometimes it hits like a wave. Either way, it pulls your mind away from peace and into fear. This prayer helps you push back, speak truth, and step into the steady presence of God.

Prayer

Father, I come to You right now, not pretending to be strong, but choosing to trust that You are. You see every thought running through my mind. You know the pressure I feel, the questions I cannot answer, and the fears that keep showing up uninvited. But I refuse to let anxiety rule me. I choose to fight it with Your truth.

I speak peace over my mind. I speak stillness over the storm. I declare that I am not abandoned. I am not forgotten. I am not at the mercy of my thoughts. You are the God who calms the wind and the waves, and You are with me now. I take every anxious thought and place it into Your hands. I will not carry what You already carried at the cross.

Replace my tension with Your strength. Replace my panic with Your presence. When my mind starts to run, remind me to pause and remember who I belong to. I do not need to see the whole plan. I just need to remember who holds it. You are the God of peace, and You have not given me a spirit of fear, but of power, love, and a sound mind.

Right now, I choose to breathe deep and trust You. I will not bow to fear. I will not surrender to pressure. I stand in faith, knowing that even if I feel shaken, I am held steady by You. My anxiety does not define me. My faith in You does. In Jesus' name, I pray. Amen.

Reflection Prompt
What specific anxious thought do I need to release to God right now?

A Prayer for Mental Clarity

"Do not conform to the pattern of this world, but be transformed by the renewing of your mind."
Romans 12:2

Confusion is one of the enemy's favorite tools. It clouds your thinking, disrupts your focus, and keeps you stuck in uncertainty. But you were not made to live in confusion. This prayer is a weapon to clear the fog and realign your thoughts with God's truth.

Prayer

God, I need clarity. My mind feels crowded. My thoughts are scattered. I struggle to focus, and I feel weighed down by decisions, distractions, and demands I cannot seem to manage. I ask You to clear the noise and bring peace to my mind. I ask You to help me see what is real and what is just pressure.

You are not the author of confusion. You are the God of truth. So I ask You to silence the lies that sound like logic. Quiet the fears that pretend to be facts. Help me separate what is urgent from what is important. Show me what to release, what to act on, and what to trust You with.

Renew my mind, Lord. Filter my thoughts through Your Word. Let every false narrative be exposed. I choose to let go of the pressure to know everything. I choose to trust that You guide my steps. Your wisdom is better than my control. You see what I cannot, and You are not confused.

Give me the ability to focus on what You are saying, not just what I am feeling. Help me to think clearly, live wisely, and speak carefully. Make my thoughts line up with Your purpose. Let my decisions come from peace, not panic.

Right now, I invite Your clarity into every part of my life. Lead me with Your Spirit. Help me move forward with confidence. I choose truth over noise, peace over pressure, and Your Word over worry. In Jesus' name, Amen.

Reflection Prompt
Where am I confusing busyness with direction, and what truth is God trying to highlight?

A Prayer for Peace Over Racing Thoughts

"You will keep in perfect peace those whose minds are steadfast, because they trust in you."
Isaiah 26:3

There are moments when your mind just won't slow down. Thoughts spin. Scenarios repeat. Fear builds momentum. In those moments, you need a reset. This prayer helps you calm the mental storm and anchor your trust in God.

Prayer

Lord, my thoughts are running ahead of me. I try to sleep, but my mind keeps working. I try to focus, but I keep drifting into what-ifs, should-haves, and worst-case outcomes. I bring my restless mind to You now. I ask You to take control of what I cannot settle on my own.

I speak stillness into this storm of thoughts. I invite Your peace into every space where stress has taken over. I release the need to have all the answers. I surrender the mental loops that steal my energy and joy. I choose to slow down and let You lead me one step at a time.

You are the God of peace, and I believe that peace is not just an idea. It is a reality I can live in when I trust You. So I turn my attention to You right now. I breathe deep. I center my heart on Your Word. I let go of control and pick up confidence. You are still in charge. You are still good. And You are right here with me.

I ask You to interrupt every thought that does not come from You. Stop the spiral. Reset my rhythm. Help me hear Your voice above the noise. Let my thoughts become still, not because everything around me is perfect, but because You are present.

Tonight, I choose rest. Tomorrow, I choose trust. Right now, I choose peace. In Jesus' name, Amen.

Reflection Prompt
What thoughts do I need to hand over to God instead of trying to solve on my own?

A Prayer to Silence Fear

"So do not fear, for I am with you. Do not be dismayed, for I am your God. I will strengthen you and help you."
Isaiah 41:10

Fear speaks loudly. It shows up in your mind, in your body, and in your choices. It tries to convince you that you are unprotected and alone. But fear has no authority when you stand in the truth of God's presence and promises. This prayer helps you confront fear directly and shut its voice down.

Prayer

Father, fear has been trying to talk to me again. It sneaks in through what I hear, what I imagine, and what I cannot control. But today I choose not to listen. I choose to silence fear with Your Word. I choose to stand in truth instead of shaking in worry.

You are with me. That is not a theory. That is my anchor. You are my strength, my shield, and my protector. I reject the idea that I am alone. I reject the thought that I am not enough. I reject the feeling that something bad is always about to happen. These are lies, and they stop here.

I speak peace to my body. I speak stillness to my mind. I speak confidence into my spirit. Fear will not lead me. Fear will not speak louder than faith. I may not know what tomorrow holds, but I know who holds me. I am not powerless. I am not exposed. I am not forgotten. You are right here, and You are not leaving.

God, help me to remember that You are stronger than what I fear. You are bigger than what I face. Let me walk with courage today—not because I feel bold, but because I know I belong to You. Let me speak with strength. Let me move forward in peace.

I declare right now that fear has no permission to speak into my life. I silence it by standing in Your truth. I take authority over every thought that brings panic, dread, or heaviness. I hand it all over to You. And I walk forward in peace, because I walk forward with You. In Jesus' name, Amen.

Reflection Prompt
What fear keeps trying to return, and what truth do I need to speak back to it?

A Prayer for Rest and Renewal

"Come to me, all you who are weary and burdened, and I will give you rest."
Matthew 11:28

You can only push for so long before the pressure wears you down. God never asked you to carry everything alone. He invites you to rest, to reset, and to let Him restore what stress has drained. This prayer is a moment to breathe, reset, and come back stronger.

Prayer

God, I am tired. Maybe not in a way others can see, but You see it. I am worn down by the weight I carry, the roles I fill, and the thoughts that never stop. I come to

You now—not to perform, not to explain, but to rest. You said I could, and I believe You.

You are not asking me to pretend I am fine. You are not impressed by how much I push through. You want me whole. You want me present. You want me restored. So I lay it all down now. The mental stress. The hidden pressure. The fear of failing. The need to hold everything together. I let it fall.

I ask You to fill me again. Fill me with Your strength. Fill me with Your peace. Let my body relax in Your presence. Let my mind unclench. Let my spirit breathe. I do not want to run on empty. I want to run on Your Spirit. I want to live refreshed.

Help me to stop treating rest like weakness. Help me see it as worship. Help me trust that You are still working even when I stop moving. I surrender the pride that says I have to prove something. I let You take the lead again.

Tonight I will sleep in peace, because You are my protector. Tomorrow I will wake with purpose, because You are my provider. Right now, I receive rest as a gift from You. I do not have to earn it. I just have to receive it. Thank You for being my safe place. In Jesus' name, Amen.

Reflection Prompt
Where am I trying to stay strong instead of letting God refill me with His peace?

Section 2: Temptation and Self-Control

A Prayer for Strength Against Sexual Sin

"Flee from sexual immorality. Do you not know that your bodies are temples of the Holy Spirit, who is in you?"
1 Corinthians 6:18–19

Sexual temptation is not a minor issue. It is one of the most aggressive spiritual attacks men face. It promises pleasure but delivers guilt, distance from God, and shame. This prayer helps you fight with truth, not willpower alone.

Prayer

Lord, You see every part of me. You know where I struggle. You know what tempts me, what catches my attention, and what draws me off track. Right now I come to You, not hiding, not pretending, but standing in the light of Your truth. I ask for strength. Not just for today, but for the moments when I feel weak and alone.

I know sexual sin is not just about the body. It starts in the mind. It grows in silence. But I choose to expose it to You now. I reject the lie that I cannot change. I reject the shame that tells me I am too far gone. I reject the cycle that says I will always fall. You have called me to freedom, and I believe You.

Help me to run from temptation, not flirt with it. Help me to protect my eyes, guard my thoughts, and turn away when compromise tries to sneak in. Let me remember that I am not just resisting sin, I am honoring You. I am guarding my future. I am protecting my purpose.

Fill my mind with what is pure. Replace images that should not be there with truth and peace. Remind me that I am not alone in this fight. Give me strength to choose what is right, even when no one is watching.

I am not a slave to lust. I am a son of the living God. I am not powerless. I am filled with the Spirit. I walk in victory, not shame. I stand today, not in fear of falling, but in the confidence that You are with me. In Jesus' name, Amen.

Reflection Prompt
What do I need to remove from my daily life to protect my purity?

A Prayer for Self-Discipline

"For the Spirit God gave us does not make us timid, but gives us power, love and self-discipline."
2 Timothy 1:7

Every man wants to grow stronger, but few succeed without discipline. It is not about perfection. It is about consistency. This prayer will help you build the spiritual muscle of self-control, one decision at a time.

Prayer

Father, I need Your help. I want to live with more focus, more order, and more purpose. I want to be the kind of man who follows through, who leads with strength, who does not drift. But I confess, it is hard. It is easy to get distracted. It is easy to start strong and then fade. I ask You to grow real discipline in me.

You have not called me to chaos. You have called me to live wisely and walk with intention. So help me today. Help me to rise with purpose, not just pressure. Help me to choose what is right, even when no one is telling me to. Help me to say no to laziness, to impulse, to the path of least resistance.

I know discipline is not a personality trait. It is a fruit of the Spirit. So I ask You to develop it in me. Give me the strength to set boundaries. Give me the focus to complete what I start. Help me not to be mastered by emotion, but to be led by truth.

When I feel like quitting, give me a second wind. When I feel scattered, bring me back to center. When I want to give in, remind me of who I am. I do not live for comfort. I live for calling. I am not here to drift. I am here to walk in purpose.

Lord, make me consistent. Make me steady. Let my yes mean yes. Let my no stand firm. Make me the kind of man who finishes what he begins, who shows up when it is hard, who lives with integrity no matter the cost. I trust You to grow this in me. In Jesus' name, Amen.

Reflection Prompt
Where in my life do I need to replace comfort with consistency?

A Prayer for Victory Over Addiction

"No temptation has overtaken you except what is common to mankind. And God is faithful. He will not let you be tempted beyond what you can bear."
1 Corinthians 10:13

Addiction tells you that you are stuck, that freedom is not possible, and that you will always return to the same pattern. But God says otherwise. This prayer helps you claim victory, not just momentary relief, but real, lasting freedom.

Prayer

God, I feel the pull. I feel the cycle trying to repeat. I feel the weight of habits that have been with me for too long. But I come to You not with shame, but with hope. I believe You are stronger than this. I believe You are my way out, not just once, but every time.

I confess my weakness, but I also confess Your strength. I do not want to live in bondage. I want to walk in freedom. I want to think clearly, choose wisely, and live boldly. I want to break this chain, not just for me, but for the people around me who need me to be whole.

Show me the lies that keep me stuck. Expose the triggers. Give me wisdom to set boundaries, and courage to reach out when I need support. Let me stop hiding. Let me start healing. You have not given me a spirit of addiction. You have given me the mind of Christ, the strength of the Spirit, and the authority to say no.

This habit does not define me. You do. This pattern is not permanent. Your power is greater. I may have fallen before, but I stand today. I choose obedience over impulse. I choose faith over flesh. I choose freedom over fear. I belong to You, and I trust You to walk with me until the chains are broken and the weight is gone.

Thank You for never giving up on me. Thank You for loving me even in the fight. I trust You for victory. In Jesus' name, Amen.

Reflection Prompt
What lie have I believed that keeps me bound, and what truth do I need to replace it with?

A Prayer to Resist Daily Temptation

"Submit yourselves, then, to God. Resist the devil, and he will flee from you."
James 4:7

Temptation does not always shout. Sometimes it whispers. It waits. It disguises itself as something harmless. That is why you must stay alert and ready. This prayer helps you stay sharp and focused in the daily battle.

Prayer

Lord, You know what I face each day. You know the areas where I am strong, and the areas where I still struggle. You know the moments where temptation tries to sneak in, disguised as something easy, something normal, something I can handle. I ask You right now to help me see clearly and respond wisely.

I do not want to play games with compromise. I do not want to flirt with decisions that slowly steal my peace. I want to walk with integrity. I want to honor You in what I look at, what I think about, what I speak, and how I live.

Give me the strength to say no when it matters. Remind me of who I am when I feel the old pull. Remind me of what I am fighting for, my future, my family, my calling. Let that be louder than the voice of temptation.

Holy Spirit, speak to me in real time. Help me feel that warning nudge when something is not right. Give me the wisdom to walk away, close the screen, leave the conversation, shut the door, or change direction. Let me respond quickly and without shame.

This is not about being perfect. This is about being committed. I am committed to growth. I am committed to holiness. I am committed to You. I will not bow to the same traps again. I stand in truth. I stand in strength. I stand with You. In Jesus' name, Amen.

Reflection Prompt
What specific temptation shows up often, and how can I prepare for it in advance?

A Prayer for Consistency in Holiness

"But just as he who called you is holy, so be holy in all you do."
1 Peter 1:15

Holiness is not about performance. It is about alignment. It is living in a way that reflects God's heart, not just in public, but in private too. This prayer helps you build consistency, even when no one is watching.

Prayer

God, I want my life to reflect You. Not just my Sunday life. Not just the parts people see. All of it. My thoughts. My habits. My choices. My words. My reactions. I want to live in a way that shows I belong to You, not for applause, but for purpose.

But I need help. It is easy to be holy for a moment. It is harder to be holy when no one sees. It is harder when I am tired, when I feel pressure, when I am tempted. So I ask You for steady strength. I ask You to build in me a holy rhythm, a pattern of obedience that becomes natural over time.

I do not want to live in extremes. I want to be consistent. I want to walk the same in private as I do in public. I want to lead from a place of integrity. I want to be the kind of man who lives clean, speaks truth, and stands firm even when it costs something.

Grow this in me, Lord. Make my heart clean. Make my steps firm. Make my words life-giving. Let my actions reflect Your character. Let my thoughts align with Your Word. I am not after perfection. I am after alignment. I am after depth. I am after more of You.

Thank You that You are patient with me. Thank You that holiness is not earned, it is received through relationship with You. Help me to stay close to You, because that is where holiness grows. I trust You to lead me. In Jesus' name, Amen.

Reflection Prompt
Where am I living in public strength but private compromise, and what needs to change?

Section 3: Isolation and Loneliness

A Prayer for God's Nearness

"The Lord is close to the brokenhearted and saves those who are crushed in spirit."
Psalm 34:18

There are days when God feels distant. The silence feels heavy. The heart feels hollow. But God's nearness is not based on feeling. It is a promise. This prayer helps you reach for Him when you cannot sense Him clearly.

Prayer

Father, I need You close. Not just the idea of You, but the nearness of You. Some days I feel like I am praying into a wall. Some nights I wonder if You hear me at all. I know the truth says You never leave, but right now I need to feel that truth deeper than my emotions.

Come near to me, Lord. Not just in theory. Come into this quiet space where I feel tired and unsure. Speak into the places where I have been trying to stay strong on the outside while feeling weak inside. I do not need more noise. I need Your voice. I need Your presence.

You said You are close to the brokenhearted. So I bring You every part of my heart that feels disconnected, overlooked, or numb. I give You the weight I have not known how to carry. I choose to believe that You are not far off, that You are right here, walking with me through the dark.

God, remind me that You are steady even when I am not. Help me to slow down long enough to notice that You are near. Let me become aware of Your presence in the ordinary. Let me hear You even in silence. Let me trust You even when I cannot see the way ahead.

Thank You for never leaving me. Thank You that I do not have to fight alone. Thank You that even when I feel distant, You are holding me closer than I realize. I trust You to meet me right here. In Jesus' name, Amen.

Reflection Prompt
Where have I mistaken God's silence for absence, and what truth do I need to remember?

A Prayer to Heal Inner Loneliness

"Be strong and courageous. Do not be afraid or terrified, for the Lord your God goes with you. He will never leave you nor forsake you."
Deuteronomy 31:6

You can be surrounded by people and still feel completely alone. Inner loneliness is not just about who is around you, but about what is going on inside you. This prayer helps you invite God into the quiet ache that no one else sees.

Prayer

Lord, there are places in me that feel empty. There are questions I carry that I have not spoken out loud. There is a quiet ache that I do not even know how to name. I bring that to You now. I invite You into the space where loneliness has taken root.

I know You see me fully. You understand what I do not know how to explain. You hear the thoughts I do not say. So I stop pretending to be fine. I stop distracting myself. I ask You to meet me right here. Not with quick fixes, but with real healing.

I ask You to speak into the part of me that feels disconnected from everything and everyone. Remind me that I am not invisible. I am not forgotten. I am not too far gone. You are the One who walks into the places that others avoid. You are the One who stays.

God, help me to stop filling my loneliness with things that do not satisfy. Help me to recognize Your nearness as more than enough. Help me to feel comfort in Your presence, even when the room is quiet and my phone is silent. You are not a distant God. You are a Father who stays close.

Heal the part of me that believes I am always on my own. Heal the old wounds that tell me connection is dangerous or that no one really understands. Teach me how to rest in You, how to open up again, and how to find my sense of belonging in Your presence first.

I trust You to fill the empty places. I trust You to heal what others could not. I trust You to remind me that I am never truly alone. In Jesus' name, Amen.

Reflection Prompt
What part of my heart have I kept hidden in loneliness that God is inviting me to open?

A Prayer to Rebuild Brotherhood

"As iron sharpens iron, so one man sharpens another." Proverbs 27:17

God never meant for men to walk through life alone. Brotherhood is not a bonus. It is a spiritual need. This prayer helps you ask God to restore connection with other men who walk in faith and strength.

Prayer

Lord, I know I was not made to live in isolation. I need brothers in the fight. I need men who will challenge me, pray for me, and remind me who I am when I forget. But I admit it has been easier to stay distant. It has been safer to stay guarded.

Help me break that pattern. Heal whatever fear or disappointment made me pull away. Help me take the risk of connection. Give me the courage to open up and the wisdom to know who to trust. I want to grow alongside men who take their walk with You seriously.

Bring people into my life who sharpen my thinking, build up my spirit, and call me higher. Show me how to be that kind of man for others too. I do not want shallow friendship. I want real brotherhood. I want the kind of loyalty that stands firm when life gets heavy.

I ask You to restore what was lost. Maybe it was trust. Maybe it was community. Maybe it was confidence in others. Whatever it was, I give it to You now. Teach me how to be present. Teach me how to listen. Teach me how to build connection that lasts.

I do not want to carry everything on my own anymore. Thank You for showing me that strength is not silence. Real strength is knowing I do not have to walk alone. In Jesus' name, Amen.

Reflection Prompt
Where have I avoided connection out of fear or pride, and what small step can I take to build real brotherhood?

A Prayer to Connect Authentically

"Therefore confess your sins to each other and pray for each other so that you may be healed."
James 5:16

You were not designed to wear a mask. Real connection happens when you stop pretending and start being real. This prayer helps you bring your full self to the table and build relationships that are honest, not just comfortable.

Prayer

God, I am tired of surface-level connection. I am tired of smiling when I am struggling. I want to live open and honest, not just with You but with the people You have placed around me. I want real friendship. I want deep connection. But I need Your help to get there.

Show me where I have been hiding. Show me where I have been afraid to be seen. Help me let go of the fear of judgment. Help me break the habit of pretending everything is fine when it is not. Give me the strength to be honest. Let my honesty invite others to be honest too.

I want friendships that are built on truth. I want connection that does not disappear when things get hard. Teach me how to be a man who listens with patience, speaks with integrity, and loves without needing to perform.

Remove the pride that keeps me quiet. Remove the shame that tells me I am the only one struggling. Remind me that there is power in speaking the truth. That healing comes when we are known and still accepted. I want that. I want to be fully known and still fully connected.

Help me build this kind of connection, one conversation at a time. One risk at a time. One moment of truth at a time. You are the God who sees me. Help me walk with others who are willing to see me too. In Jesus' name, Amen.

Reflection Prompt
What mask have I been wearing, and what would it look like to show up without it?

A Prayer to Feel Seen and Known

"You have searched me, Lord, and you know me."
Psalm 139:1

Every man longs to be seen for who he truly is and still be accepted. Not for performance. Not for appearance. But for the soul underneath it all. This prayer helps you open up to the One who knows you completely and teaches you how to receive love without earning it.

Prayer

Lord, there are moments when I wonder if anyone truly sees me. Not the version I show, not the strong front I carry, but the man underneath it all. The man who is tired. The man who still carries things he has not talked about. The man who wants to be known but does not always know how to open up.

You see me. You know me. You formed every part of me. You are not surprised by what I feel. You are not ashamed of where I struggle. You are not pulling away. You are leaning in. And I choose right now to believe that.

I ask You to help me live in the confidence of being fully known. I do not want to keep proving myself. I do not want to keep performing to be accepted. I want to rest in the truth that I am already loved by You.

And Lord, I ask You to bring people into my life who see me too. Not just what I do, but who I am. Help me build friendships where I am safe to be honest. Help me become the kind of man who sees others with that same depth and grace.

I do not need to shout to be seen. I do not need to earn it. I am already known. I am already held. I am already chosen by You. Thank You for never overlooking me. Thank You for reminding me that even in silence, I am seen. In Jesus' name, Amen.

Reflection Prompt
What part of me have I been hiding in fear of rejection, and how is God inviting me to be fully known?

Section 4: Family and Leadership

A Prayer for Your Role as a Husband

"Husbands, love your wives, just as Christ loved the church and gave Himself up for her."
Ephesians 5:25

Being a husband is not about control. It is about service, strength, and sacrifice. This prayer helps you ask God to shape your heart and leadership in a way that honors Him and uplifts your wife.

Prayer

God, I thank You for the gift of marriage and the responsibility You have given me as a husband. I admit I do not always know what I am doing. I do not always lead with patience. I do not always love with the kind of consistency I should. But I want to grow. I want to become the kind of man who reflects Your heart in my home.

Help me love her with humility and strength. Teach me how to listen. Teach me how to stay calm when emotions run high. Help me set the spiritual tone in my house. Let my words bring life. Let my actions bring peace. Let my presence be one of protection and encouragement.

If I have caused harm with my silence, my pride, or my anger, I ask for Your grace to heal and restore. Break any selfishness that keeps me from loving fully. Help me serve her without keeping score. Show me what it means to lay down my life for her daily, not just in words but in choices.

Fill me with wisdom when I feel unsure. Remind me that leadership does not mean dominance. It means responsibility. It means standing in the gap. It means staying present. I want to be faithful in the small things. I want to be steady even when life gets messy.

Thank You for trusting me with this role. I cannot do it in my own strength. I need You to shape me every day into the husband You've called me to be. In Jesus' name, Amen.

Reflection Prompt
What does my wife need from me right now that I may be avoiding, delaying, or overlooking?

A Prayer for Future Fatherhood or Father Healing

"He will turn the hearts of the fathers to their children, and the hearts of the children to their fathers."
Malachi 4:6

Whether you are a father, long to be one, or are healing from wounds caused by one, this prayer creates space to meet God as a Father and to prepare your heart for generational healing and leadership.

Prayer

Father, I bring You my story. All of it. Whether I had a good example or none at all, whether I am a dad now or still waiting for that chapter, I surrender this part of my life to You. You are the perfect Father, and I want to learn from You.

If I carry wounds from my own father, I ask You to heal them. If there are words that broke me or silences that left me lost, I give them to You now. Help me forgive where I need to forgive. Help me release bitterness that poisons my present. I do not want the past to shape my future.

And if You are calling me into fatherhood, prepare me. Build patience in me. Build courage. Build joy. Let me be the kind of father who speaks life, who protects fiercely, who shows affection without hesitation. Let me pass on blessing, not burden. Strength, not shame.

Help me become the man my children can rely on. Help me stay when things get hard. Help me model faith, love, and honor, even when I am tired or frustrated. I ask You to shape my legacy, not by my effort but by Your Spirit working through me.

No matter what my story has been, I choose to begin again. I choose to step forward, not with fear, but with hope. You are redeeming what I thought was lost. You are writing a new story through me. And I trust You with every page of it. In Jesus' name, Amen.

Reflection Prompt
What message about fatherhood have I been carrying that God may want to replace?

A Prayer to Lead Spiritually at Home

"But as for me and my house, we will serve the Lord."
Joshua 24:15

Leadership in the home does not start with shouting orders or being the loudest voice. It begins with consistency, humility, and a heart that follows God first. This prayer helps you take up your spiritual authority as the one who sets the tone of faith in your household.

Prayer

God, You have placed me in this home for a reason. Not just to provide or protect, but to lead spiritually. I admit there are days I do not know how to do that. I do not always feel qualified. Sometimes I feel like I am still figuring it out myself. But I believe You equip those You call, and I want to grow into this role.

Help me be the one who brings prayer into the day. Help me open the Word when things feel unclear. Help me speak blessing over my family and build habits that bring us closer to You. Let my leadership be steady, not controlling. Let it invite trust, not fear.

When I want to stay passive or distracted, wake me up. Help me be intentional. Help me notice where my home needs spiritual covering. Help me take the first step, even if no one else follows at first. Give me wisdom to lead my wife, my children, and even myself with grace and direction.

Let the atmosphere of my home shift because I choose to walk with You. Let peace take the place of tension. Let truth replace confusion. Let worship rise where stress once ruled. And above all, let love be the loudest thing in our home.

Thank You for trusting me with this sacred responsibility. Teach me daily. Guide me gently. And build my house on a foundation that will not shake. In Jesus' name, Amen.

Reflection Prompt
What spiritual habit could I start today that would change the atmosphere of my home?

A Prayer to Break Generational Patterns

"See, I am doing a new thing! Now it springs up; do you not perceive it?"
Isaiah 43:19

Every man has a history, but in Christ, you are not bound to repeat what you came from. This prayer invites God to break harmful cycles and establish a new legacy through you.

Prayer

God, You see what runs through my bloodline. You see the pain, the habits, the strongholds, the things no one talks about but everyone carries. And I believe You did not bring me this far to repeat what broke me. I believe You are the God who makes all things new.

If there is anger that has passed from father to son, break it. If addiction has haunted my family line, break it. If pride, abuse, fear, or silence have shaped the men before me, I ask You to interrupt that pattern with me. I do not want to pass on pain. I want to pass on peace.

Show me what needs to stop here. Show me what needs to start with me. Let me be a man who rewrites the story, not just for myself, but for those who come after me. I want to build a legacy that speaks of freedom, not bondage. Of blessing, not burden.

Give me the courage to face what others ignored. Give me the honesty to name what needs healing. And give me the strength to live differently, even when it is hard. You are doing something new, and I choose to say yes.

Let my life be the place where cycles end and new beginnings rise. Let what once felt impossible become my testimony. Thank You for giving me the authority to close doors that have been open too long. In Jesus' name, Amen.

Reflection Prompt
What pattern do I see in my family line that I do not want to pass down?

A Prayer for Unity and Peace in the Household

"If a house is divided against itself, that house cannot stand."
Mark 3:25

A divided home becomes a place of tension and weariness, but a home centered on God can be a sanctuary of peace. This prayer helps you invite the Holy Spirit to restore unity and bring calm to every room in your house.

Prayer

Father, I lift up my home to You. Every room. Every relationship. Every word spoken and unspoken. You know what goes on behind closed doors. You see the moments of tension, the miscommunication, the stress, the things we try to hide from others. And You care.

I ask You to bring peace where there is conflict. Bring understanding where there is misunderstanding. Bring patience where there has been frustration. Teach us to speak to one another with honor. Teach us to listen before we react. Help us slow down long enough to choose love over pride.

If there is bitterness growing beneath the surface, pull it up by the roots. If there is unforgiveness in our words or silence, shine Your light on it. Let nothing toxic stay hidden. Let nothing broken stay untouched.

I ask You to make this home a safe place. A place where faith is felt. A place where laughter can return. A place where healing happens daily, not just occasionally. Let peace be the language of our home. Let unity be the atmosphere. Let love be the rule.

Thank You that Your Spirit can do what we cannot. You can soften hearts. You can restore connection. You can calm storms that feel too loud. I invite You to do that here and now. In Jesus' name, Amen.

Reflection Prompt
What can I do today to be a peacemaker in my home, not just a peacekeeper?

Section 5: Spiritual Fatigue and Pressure

A Prayer for Strength When You Feel Weak

"My grace is sufficient for you, for My power is made perfect in weakness."
2 Corinthians 12:9

There are moments when your strength runs out. Not just physical strength, but emotional and spiritual strength too. This prayer is for the days you feel like you have nothing left, and yet you choose to call on the One whose strength never runs dry.

Prayer

God, I feel tired. Not just in body, but in my soul. I have been carrying weight I was never meant to carry alone. I have tried to be strong for others, to keep it together, to stay focused, to press on. But today I admit I feel weak. And I need You.

Thank You that You do not reject me in my weakness. You do not look down on me when I am worn out. You draw near. You remind me that Your power is made perfect in moments like this. I do not have to pretend. I do not have to push past my limits. I simply have to lean on You.

Help me release the pressure to perform. Help me let go of the pride that says I must have it all figured out. Teach me how to rest in Your strength, not just talk about it. I do not want to live on empty anymore.

Fill me with Your Spirit right now. Let courage rise again. Let peace replace panic. Let clarity replace confusion. Let Your voice be louder than the noise around me. Remind me that You are with me, not just when I feel strong, but especially when I feel broken.

I receive Your grace for today. I trust You to carry me through this moment. And I believe that even in this weakness, You are doing something good in me. In Jesus' name, Amen.

Reflection Prompt
What is one area of my life where I am trying to be strong on my own instead of relying on God?

A Prayer When You Feel Spiritually Dry

"Blessed are those who hunger and thirst for righteousness, for they will be filled."
Matthew 5:6

There are seasons when your soul feels dry, when prayer feels distant, and Scripture feels silent. This is not failure. This is an invitation to seek God more deeply. This prayer gives you words when you are thirsty for more but do not know how to ask.

Prayer

Father, I come to You feeling empty. Not because I doubt You, but because I miss You. I have not felt connected in a while. I go through the motions. I show up, I pray, I read, but it feels dry. I long to feel Your presence again. I want to be filled.

If there is anything blocking me from experiencing You, show me. If I have allowed distraction, sin, or busyness to build a wall between us, help me tear it down. I do not want to fake passion. I want the real thing. I want intimacy with You, not just information about You.

Stir my hunger again. Awaken my thirst. Give me a deeper desire for prayer, not just routine. Let Your Word come alive to me again. Let worship feel like a connection, not a chore. Let my time with You shift from duty to desire.

I know You are not far. I know You have not turned Your back. Even now, You are drawing me closer. Even now, You are whispering my name. Help me slow down long enough to hear You. Help me quiet the noise so I can receive again.

Thank You that You are faithful, even when I feel distant. Thank You that You promise to fill those who hunger and thirst. I say yes to that promise now. Fill me again, Lord. Renew me. Revive me. Reignite what has gone dim. In Jesus' name, Amen.

Reflection Prompt
What is one small step I can take this week to reconnect with God in a personal way?

A Prayer for Patience Under Pressure

"Let perseverance finish its work so that you may be mature and complete, not lacking anything."
James 1:4

Pressure has a way of revealing what is inside you. And sometimes, in the middle of deadlines, conflict, or waiting seasons, patience wears thin. This prayer is for the man who wants to stay grounded, not reactive, even when the weight feels heavy.

Prayer

God, I feel the pressure. It's coming from all sides. Responsibilities at work, expectations at home, things I can't control, and problems I don't have quick answers for. I feel my patience running out. I feel the tension building inside me. But I know You are not a God of panic. You are a God of peace.

Help me not react out of frustration. Help me slow down instead of snap. Teach me how to pause and pray before I act. I want to be steady in the middle of the storm, not swept up by it. I want to carry Your presence even when life pushes hard.

Grow my patience, not just in silence, but in attitude. Help me trust Your timing. Help me let go of the need to fix everything instantly. Help me see that what feels like delay is often the space where You are doing something deeper in me.

Let pressure produce perseverance. Let hard moments shape something holy in me. I want to come out of this season with more faith, not more frustration. With more peace, not more regret.

Thank You that You are not rushing me, and You are not overwhelmed by what I carry. I give You the pressure, the tension, and the urge to control. Give me Your patience in return. In Jesus' name, Amen.

Reflection Prompt
What pressure point in my life needs a different attitude and a slower response?

A Prayer for Focus and Mental Fortitude

"Set your minds on things above, not on earthly things."
Colossians 3:2

In a world full of distractions, your focus is one of your greatest spiritual weapons. When your mind is all over the place, so is your spirit. This prayer centers you and builds strength to stay locked into what matters most.

Prayer

Father, I confess that my mind has been scattered. I try to concentrate, but distractions pull me every direction. My thoughts race, my worries multiply, and my focus fades. I need You to renew my mind today. I need clarity, strength, and discipline in my thinking.

Help me block out the noise. Help me say no to the unnecessary. Help me recognize what steals my attention and drains my energy. I do not want to waste my mind on things that do not grow me, shape me, or bring me closer to You.

Sharpen my thinking. Strengthen my will. Train me to stay mentally locked into what You are doing, not just what is urgent or loud. Let me be a man of depth, not distraction. Give me the mental fortitude to follow through, even when I do not feel like it.

Remind me that discipline is spiritual. That focus is an act of worship. That You gave me a mind not to drift, but to direct toward Your truth. Today, I choose to think with purpose. I choose to be present. I choose to silence the lies and anchor in Your voice.

Thank You for giving me the ability to train my thoughts. Thank You that You have not given me a spirit of fear, but of power, love, and a sound mind. I receive that today. In Jesus' name, Amen.

Reflection Prompt
What distraction do I need to remove to sharpen my focus on what God has assigned me?

A Prayer to Guard Your Peace at Work

"You will keep in perfect peace those whose minds are steadfast, because they trust in You."
Isaiah 26:3

Work is where many battles begin. It is where tension builds, comparison starts, and burnout can creep in. This prayer helps you invite God into your workplace and protect your peace from whatever may come.

Prayer

God, I bring my workplace to You. Every meeting, every task, every interaction. You know what I am walking into today. You know the pressure, the personalities, the potential conflicts. And I ask that You guard my peace through it all.

Help me remember that I work for You first. That my worth is not in my performance, title, or paycheck. That no matter what happens around me, I can carry calm within me. I choose to be a man of peace in a place of pressure.

Cover my mind from stress. Cover my heart from offense. Cover my soul from exhaustion. Let me walk into that space with Your presence, not my panic. Let me bring solutions, not strife. Let me be a man others trust because they can sense something different in me.

If conflict arises, give me wisdom. If my efforts go unseen, give me security in You. If I feel stretched too thin, remind me to pause and breathe with You. I do not want to just survive the day. I want to carry light into it.

Thank You that I do not enter the workplace alone. You are with me. You go before me. You give me strength to work with excellence and peace to walk away without weight. I receive that now. In Jesus' name, Amen.

Reflection Prompt
How can I bring peace into my workplace environment today, regardless of circumstances?

Section 6: Direct Spiritual Warfare

A Prayer to Break Spiritual Strongholds

"For the weapons of our warfare are not of the flesh but have divine power to destroy strongholds."
2 Corinthians 10:4

Strongholds are more than habits. They are patterns of thinking, spiritual chains, and internal battles that resist God's truth. This prayer is for the man who refuses to let bondage define his future.

Prayer

Lord, I recognize that there are strongholds in my life. Thought patterns that keep cycling. Lies that keep whispering. Behaviors that keep repeating. I am tired of feeling stuck. I am ready for breakthrough.

You said the weapons You give us are not weak. They are powerful. They are spiritual. And they are enough to tear down whatever has tried to keep me in chains. Right now, I name the stronghold that needs to fall. I bring it into the light of Your truth.

I break agreement with lies I have believed for too long. Lies about who I am, lies about my worth, lies about what I will never change. In the name of Jesus, I renounce every thought that exalts itself against the knowledge of God.

I choose to believe what You say, not what my past says, not what fear says, not what failure says. I take every thought captive right now and submit it to You. No stronghold is too big for You. No chain is too heavy. You are the Deliverer.

Tear down what has tried to stand in Your way. Burn up every root that does not come from You. Let freedom flood my heart, my mind, and my decisions. This is not just self-improvement. This is spiritual war. And by Your power, I declare the stronghold broken. In Jesus' name, Amen.

Reflection Prompt
What specific stronghold has tried to define me, and what truth from God do I need to replace it with?

A Prayer to Cancel the Enemy's Assignment

"No weapon formed against you shall prosper, and you will refute every tongue that accuses you."
Isaiah 54:17

The enemy is strategic. He aims to steal your focus, your peace, your relationships, and your identity. But God has given you authority to shut down those plans. This prayer cancels every spiritual assignment set against you.

Prayer

Father, I come to You with full confidence in who You are. You are the One who exposes darkness and breaks the power of the enemy. Right now, I take my position in the Spirit and cancel every assignment the enemy has launched against my life.

Any attack on my mind, I declare void. Any plan to divide my relationships, I render powerless. Any voice of accusation, I silence with the blood of Jesus. No scheme, no curse, no weapon will prosper against me because I am covered by Your covenant.

I take authority over anything that has tried to confuse, distract, or derail me. I reject the spirit of fear. I rebuke the spirit of heaviness. I close every open door I have allowed, knowingly or unknowingly. Cleanse my heart, my home, and my habits.

I ask for divine protection over my family, my calling, and my future. Assign angels to surround and defend what belongs to You. Let every attempt of the enemy backfire and become a testimony of Your power. I do not walk in fear. I walk in faith.

Thank You for giving me the right to stand strong. I do not need to fight for victory. I fight from victory. The battle is already won. I just step into the authority You have already given me. In Jesus' name, Amen.

Reflection Prompt
Where in my life do I sense the enemy is attacking, and how can I speak God's authority into that situation today?

A Prayer for Angelic Protection

"For He will command His angels concerning you to guard you in all your ways."
Psalm 91:11

You are not fighting alone. Heaven assigns protection when you walk in obedience. This prayer invites God's angelic defense into every area of your life.

Prayer

Lord, I thank You that I am never alone. Even when I cannot see it, You are guarding me. You have assigned heavenly forces to cover me, surround me, and go before me. I ask now for angelic protection over every area of my life.

Guard my coming and my going. Guard the doorways of my home and the pathways of my future. Send angels to stand at the borders of my relationships, my decisions, and my dreams. I refuse to live in fear when You have given me a covering.

I speak protection over my mind and thoughts. Over my sleep and rest. Over my family and my children. Over every place I set my foot today. I do not look to superstition or luck. I look to the God who commands angels with precision and love.

Block every attack before it forms. Redirect every trap before I step into it. Scatter every plan of darkness before it reaches my door. Let Your heavenly warriors fight for me where I cannot see. I receive Your covering not just for survival, but for victory.

Thank You, Father, for surrounding me with more than I can imagine. Thank You that I do not need to fear spiritual battles when I am under Your protection. I trust You completely. In Jesus' name, Amen.

Reflection Prompt
What area of my life do I need to invite God's supernatural protection into more intentionally?

A Prayer to Walk in Authority

"I have given you authority to trample on snakes and scorpions and to overcome all the power of the enemy."
Luke 10:19

You were never meant to live as a passive believer. God has given you real authority. This prayer is about stepping into that truth with boldness and clarity.

Prayer

Father, I have too often lived like a man without power. I have tolerated what You never told me to accept. But now I rise up and take hold of what You have already given me. You have placed authority in me, and today I choose to walk in it.

I speak Your word with boldness. I reject every lie that says I am weak, helpless, or stuck. I have been given power through Christ to stand firm, speak truth, and push back darkness. I do not shrink back from battle. I rise in confidence.

Let my words carry weight. Let my prayers carry fire. Let my presence in every room shift the spiritual atmosphere. Not because I am great, but because You live in me. I carry Your name, Your Spirit, and Your victory.

Teach me how to use what You have entrusted to me. Give me wisdom to discern when to speak and when to stand. Show me how to pray not just for protection, but from position. Remind me daily that I do not need to ask for what I already have.

Thank You for the authority that flows from sonship. I do not have to earn it. I only need to walk in it. I say yes to the role You have placed on my shoulders. I choose spiritual courage over spiritual passivity. In Jesus' name, Amen.

Reflection Prompt
Where have I been acting powerless in a situation where God has given me authority?

A Prayer for Full Deliverance

"So if the Son sets you free, you will be free indeed."
John 8:36

Deliverance is not about a one-time escape. It is about permanent freedom from bondage. This prayer invites the Holy Spirit to bring full release and cleansing from anything that has tried to keep you in chains.

Prayer

Jesus, You are my Deliverer. You do not just rescue me. You set me free completely. And today, I ask for full deliverance. Not partial healing. Not temporary relief. I want complete freedom in body, mind, and spirit.

I invite Your Holy Spirit to go into the deepest places. To expose what still holds me. To uproot what still affects me. To break what still tries to bind me. I give You full access. Shine Your light in every hidden place.

I renounce every spirit that is not from You. Every influence, every agreement, every lie, every curse. I cancel their right to operate in my life. I repent for anything I've allowed that gave darkness a foothold. And I shut those doors now, in Jesus' name.

Fill me with Your Spirit. Wash every part of me clean. Rewire my thoughts. Renew my emotions. Restore my body. Realign my identity. I do not want to just be rescued from sin. I want to be established in freedom.

Let the chains fall off. Let the cycles break. Let the weight lift. Deliver me from anything that has tried to define me outside of You. I receive the freedom that Jesus paid for in full. I receive it now. In Jesus' name, Amen.

Reflection Prompt
What does full freedom look like for me, and what might still need to be surrendered to receive it?

Chapter 3 – Reflection and Spiritual Activation

3.1 Don't Just Pray, Listen

Prayer is not a one-way street. Too often as men, we approach it like a task list, speak our words, unload our concerns, ask for help, then move on. But the true power of spiritual warfare prayer lies not only in what we say to God, but in our willingness to listen to what He says back.

God is not silent. He is not distant. He is not just a divine receiver of information. He is a speaking Father who responds, guides, convicts, affirms, and leads. Every time you pray, there is an invitation to slow down and hear.

You were not built just to speak. You were built to discern. Real spiritual maturity begins when you don't just know how to cry out, but when you learn how to receive direction, correction, and revelation in the quiet.

Hearing God's voice does not always mean an audible sound. For many, it comes as a deep inner knowing, a thought you didn't create, a scripture that lights up suddenly, a peace that interrupts confusion, or a nudge in your spirit you can't explain. His voice is often more familiar than we realize, but we drown it out with busyness, noise, and control.

When you pray each of the warfare prayers in this book, take a few minutes afterward to remain still. Ask God, "What do You want to show me about this?" Then listen. Do not rush. Do not force. Just sit in the awareness that He is near and wants to respond.

The discipline of listening creates a space for transformation. What you hear may not always be what you want, but it will be what you need. Sometimes God will expose something hidden. Sometimes He will bring comfort. Other times He will prompt you to act. His voice will never contradict His Word, but it will often cut through excuses and guide you straight into alignment.

If you struggle to hear anything, do not assume you are doing it wrong. Spiritual hearing is sharpened through use. Think of it like training a muscle. The more you slow down and listen, the more sensitive you become. Do not base your faith on feelings. Base it on the truth that He promises to speak.

"My sheep hear my voice," Jesus said. You are His. And that means you have access to that voice. You may not always recognize it immediately, but you will learn. Ask Him to make it clear. Write down what you sense. Revisit it later. Over time, you will see patterns, confirmations, and growth.

You are not just a man who talks to God. You are a man who walks with Him. That means you walk in conversation. In relationship. In rhythm. And that starts by being willing to hear, not just in crisis, not just when desperate, but daily.

Let this chapter serve as your reminder that spiritual warfare is not about shouting louder. It is about discerning deeper. The enemy does not fear volume. He fears clarity. A man who hears God is a man who cannot be manipulated. A man who hears God is a man who walks in alignment and power.

So the next time you finish a prayer, pause. Stay still. Close your eyes. Say, "Speak, Lord, I'm listening." And trust that He will.

3.2 Journal Prompts for Men After Each Prayer

Prayer is only the beginning. If you want lasting transformation, you need to process what is shifting inside of you. That's why journaling after each prayer matters. It isn't about being a good writer or expressing emotions perfectly. It's about getting honest with God and with yourself.

A man who doesn't reflect is a man who repeats. And the enemy counts on you staying reactive, rushed, and unaware. But when you slow down to write, you make space for clarity. You notice patterns. You uncover what God is working on. You remember the victories and identify the battles still ahead.

These prompts are designed to help you engage with each prayer at a deeper level. They will help you track your growth, recognize your blind spots, and hear God more clearly over time. You don't need to answer all of them every day. Choose one or two that stir something in you and let your response flow naturally.

Use these prompts after each prayer in Chapter 2. You can keep a notebook, a dedicated journal, or even type into your phone. The method does not matter. What matters is that you show up with honesty, even if it's raw, even if you don't feel spiritual, even if all you can write is a sentence or two. That's enough to open the door for transformation.

Here are your go-to reflection questions:

What stood out most in this prayer today?
Did a certain phrase hit you harder than others? Was there a part that made you uncomfortable or deeply resonated? Write it down.

What am I sensing God is highlighting in me?
Is He calling attention to something you've ignored, avoided, or buried? Is He pointing to a change He wants to make in your mindset or habits?

What emotion came up during the prayer?
Don't dismiss your emotions. They reveal what's going on beneath the surface. Were you angry, afraid, hopeful, numb? Start there and explore it.

Where in my life do I need this prayer to show up right now?
Make it specific. Don't just pray for peace in general. Is it peace at work? In your marriage? In your thoughts when you lie in bed at night?

What truth do I need to remember this week?
Let this become your anchor. Is God reminding you that you are not alone? That you have authority? That you are loved and not forgotten?

What step is God asking me to take?
Prayer is not just emotional relief. It's meant to activate you. Is there someone you need to forgive? A habit you need to break? A conversation you've been avoiding?

Where do I see progress, even if it's small?
Celebrate it. Spiritual growth often shows up in subtle

ways, a calmer reaction, a clearer mind, a better choice. Don't overlook them.

What does surrender look like today?
Each prayer calls you to lay something down. Identify it. Name what you need to release, give up, or stop controlling.

Did I hear or sense anything from God after the prayer?
Maybe it was a scripture that came to mind, a picture, a phrase, or just a sense of peace. Write it down, even if it feels unclear.

Is there a pattern in my responses across multiple days?
Over time, look back at what you've written. Are the same issues coming up? Is God leading you through a theme or deeper healing?

This practice isn't just about looking inward. It's about creating space for the Holy Spirit to guide your inner world. The more intentional you are, the more fruit you'll see. You'll begin to recognize the hand of God in your everyday life. You'll feel less lost and more grounded. You'll stop drifting through days and start engaging with them on purpose.

Be faithful to this process. Some days will feel dry. Others will feel like a breakthrough. But every time you write, you make space for something new to take root. That's what makes a man dangerous in the kingdom, a man who is not just praying, but paying attention.

Standing Firm in Every Battle

You've now walked through the essential tools of spiritual warfare, understanding the battlefield, wielding prayer as your first weapon, declaring God's truth, and activating real change through reflection. This is not the end. It's the beginning. You are stepping into a stronger, more aware, more spiritually equipped version of yourself.

Remember this: strength is not about perfection. It's about perseverance. It's not about never struggling. It's about never giving up. What you've built here—day by day, prayer by prayer, insight by insight—is the foundation of a life anchored in God's power. It will not only protect you, but it will also shape every area of your life: your home, your relationships, your work, your purpose.

Your battleground stretches beyond these pages. It continues in your thoughts, your rhythms, and your routines. But now you have daily prayers shaped by scripture, spiritual reflections to sharpen your heart, and the awareness to walk with authority. No matter what comes your way, you can stand firm.

To equip you even further, download the additional resources designed for men like you—tools that reinforce your daily practice, support deeper growth, and keep you activated in real time. These tools are ready for you to use, they've been crafted to fit into the life God is building in you.

Stand strong. Stay close to Him. Keep praying. Keep reflecting. Keep walking in bold spiritual authority. The journey will not always be easy. But it will always be worth it. You are chosen. You are called. You are covered. And you are not alone.

Scan the QR code or go to the link below to download all the bonuses:

bit.ly/spiritualwarfarebonusformen

www.ingramcontent.com/pod-product-compliance
Lightning Source LLC
Chambersburg PA
CBHW060353240825
31572CB00013B/933